Poetry for the variable

D. S. Duke

BookLeaf
Publishing

India | USA | UK

Presentation by *BookLeaf Publishing*

Web: www.bookleafpub.com

E-mail: info@bookleafpub.com

ISBN: 978-93-5744-928-1

First edition 2022

Bloody dancefloor

Another Night, Another Dance,

and another partner, of course.

I often wonder what makes me come to this
place,

night after night,

day by day,

like I'm entrapped by an unknown force.

Could the scenery be the cause,

the dance floor changes each time.

At times it's a grassy green,

a rocky gray,

yellow as beach sand,

woody as a forest,

cold and white as frozen powder

hard as a city street,

or as wet as the sea;

and for all its dance floors,

this place only has two lights.

One called Sun.

The other, Moon.

This place's ceiling changes just as much as the floor.

Four forms I have witnessed so far

A blue top sometimes accompanied by white masses, usually with the sunlight.

A beautiful orange-red overhead, which usually occurs when one light switches with the other.

A dark, mysterious black top, sometimes with white crystals and the moonlight, or pieces of it.

A gray top usually accompanied by water, ice crystals, electricity, high-velocity force of air, and booming sounds.

No…

No…it is not the multiple scenes that make me come.

This leaves the only other factor.

The excitement.

The excitement that erupts on the dancefloor of This place called earth.

This soon-to-be bloody dancefloor!

Yes..The dance that is old as earth and survived the times,

and changes with this place.

Yes, an exhilarating dance it is.

A dance of life and death,

A dance of energy,

A dance of destruction,

A dance of honor.

At times it's a clashing of blades,

At other times a hail of bullets,

At its rawest form, an exchange of hands and
feet,

a collision of bodies.

it's a dance fueled by emotion and ideas,

It brings out one strength and skills,

and pushes one's self to the brink.

Yes…this is why I come here,

day by day,

night by night.

To feel the excitement,

To be engulfed in the emotion,

To succumb to the experience.

To dance the dance known as Battle

on my bloody dancefloor.

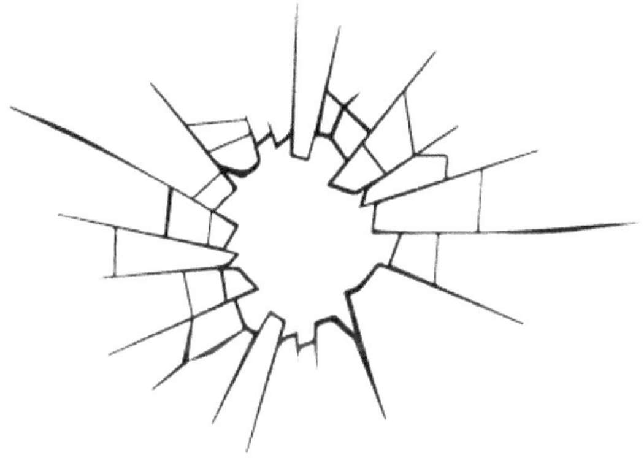

Comply

How many of you got the talk from your moms
and dads?

Not the sex talk, the birds and the bees,

But the one that protects you from police
brutality.

The comply talk, guidelines for colored people

when encountering the boys in blue.

Always answer with sir or mam

To any questions or commands

Always do what they ask

No matter how insulting task,

Do whatever you can to be perceived as a threat

You won't end up dead.

Fair advice, but there's a slight problem with it

I'm a male with beautiful dark skin, brown eyes, and full lips

I'm also 5'10 and weigh 266

I'm a 'threat' cause I fucking exist

But still, my parents' advice is to comply

Best chance to survive

Still can't help but think I'm still might die

My life on the line

Answer with sir and mam

Listen to their commands

Even if it leads to me on the floor

Knees to my neck, hands behind my back

Do whatever they ask

No matter the task

Hopefully, when I reach for my ID

My chest won't get blast

Do whatever you can to not be perceived as a
threat

And you won't end up dead.

So can't wear hoodies, walk into my home, play
outside, live my life

You know things that might label me as criminal
in their head

Even if I do follow the cops,

There is still a chance my heart might stop

Forced onto the street

While they take my ability to breath

And no, I not blaming all police

I know not all you are bad

But there's enough of you

That'll pull the trigger even if I raise my hands,
unarmed and ask you not to shoot

It's because of that every time that damn badge
is near

I can't help the thoughts born from exhausted
tears

That I might become another lost life

Even if I comply.

I.M.P.E.R.F.E.C.T

I am

Immeasurable.

Myriad.

Perpetual.

Expanse.

Remarkably limitless.

Futurity.

Excelling in life.

Continuous.

Term-less.

I am Imperfect; I am limitless and endless.

I am not

Prescribed.

Ending.

Restricted.

Finite.

Exclusive.

Confined.

Tenured.

I have no limit, no barrier, no stopping point. I
am not perfect.

Defeat

Defeat.
Oh, it's so humbling, isn't it?
Nothing in the world
Test and teaches us like defeat.

Greatest stories of success
Initiates from lofty losses, you know.
Victories stolen from its maws inspire
Everyone who hears them for eras.

Up to you, though, let your current defeat
Put down for good or buckle down, stand and
?

It flares

It flares...

every now and then...

It flares...

Like spikes through his back and hair.

When he feels lost, alone, weak, and scared...

…it flares

…when his eyes unwittingly tear

…it flares

…but it's ok

…cause she's there

…caressing his spikes and hair

..she's there

..holding him as he voices fears

..she's there

..whispering words of encouragement, pride, and love in his ear

..she's there

..it retracts the flares

..helps his mind and heart clear

..hearing her own heart in his ear

…knowing her valorous love is near

..it retracts the flares.

Knowing that she was and always will be there.

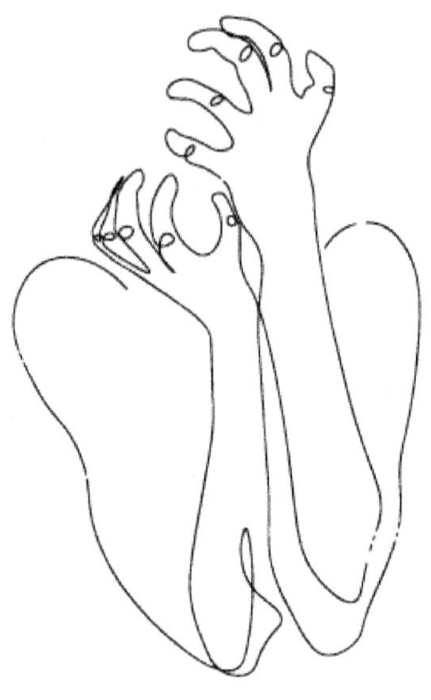

Thug and Tree fairy

Their first meeting was something.

The stars were out that night.
Something you can't see with the city lights.

So, He made his way to the large tree.
On the hill overlooking the city.

The same trip he made a few times a week.
Even before he was running the streets.

He came to look at the city, his kingdom, his
home.
With food, a drink, headphones, time alone.

He was expecting it just to be him and the tree.
That's why he was surprised to see, she.

Yellow and orange swirls in the hair of leaf
green.
Skin the color of bark from the peach tree.

A statuesque form under a knee-length gown.
Sultry eyes and lips of a gentle brown.

She looked at him, her wing fluttered, and her eyes became teary.
Before smiling and introducing herself as the tree fairy.

Their first meeting was exciting.

She grew with him completely unknown.
Cloaked by magic, a guardian shadow.

She watched him make the trek countless times.
To make sure that tree, her avatar, not live, but strive.

She heard his goals, his troubles, his future plans.
Watched as life broke a warm pure boy to make a cold, powerful man.

Powerful he was physically, emotionally, and mentally.
With limbs, eyes, and skin dark and thick as an oak tree.

Yet, despite how cold and thuggish society made him be.
He still makes his trips to her and the tree.

With those of brown eyes and kissable lips.

She can't help that his smiles make her heart
skips.

That his voice makes her mush.
His style makes her blush.

How she wanted to hug her 'thug.'
Especially on the days when he had it rough.

That before she knew it, like fruit from a tree.
She was in love with the thug; the boy grew to
be.

It is why she cried when he looked at her for the
first time.
The shock and surprise gleam his eye.

And her body moved in a rush.
Cause she can finally...finally hold her thug.

Two minutes

It take her two minutes to brush her teeth.

In that two minutes, she came to a conclusion.

Among the brushing of her maw, she thought clearly.

About her Life, about her goals, about her wants...

About them, the person lying in her bed.

The arms she silently crawled out of to not awaken.

She spat out the paste and got a cup of mouthwash, swishing it.

She thought about their past. Full with times good, bad, horrifying, amazing.

Magical...Oh, so magical.

The drama with their family.

The trauma it caused them.

The fact they overcame all of it.

She thought of failed proposals, reassuring promises, disillusioned dreams, and the new path she's on.

The new path they are on.

The cohabitation between her and her 'much more' than best friend.

She spat out the mouthwash, getting a cap of water.

She thought about the future...

What she wants from it...

Who she wants in it and how.

She spat out the water and looked at their reflection, licking their teeth.

Feeling refreshed and convinced...

Hearing the groans of their other as they woke,
they walked over and greeted them by climbing
upon them as they always did.

Looking at their smiling face with one of
determination they spoke.

"Let's get married."

Two minutes...She came to a conclusion.

Anger

Anger gets a bad rap.

Most people fear anger.

They fear the heat of it.

The surge of it.

The overwhelming power and addictive adrenaline it can bring.

To be consumed by it.

You know the saying, "Anger doesn't solve anything, builds nothing, but can destroy everything."

This is a lie.

Anger is an emotion.

Emotion is power.

Power is a tool.

A tool that reveals its wielder intention.

It has no agency.

No purpose.

No intention...Except for its users.

Anger doesn't do anything by itself.

It doesn't consume us; we consume it.

It doesn't surge of us; it surges within us.

We do not power it; we're powered by it.

Anger can't destroy, hate, burn, retaliate, revolt.

It can't fight, rebel, revolt, build or cause change.

Anger doesn't get things done.

Angry people do...So what are you waiting for?

Get angry.

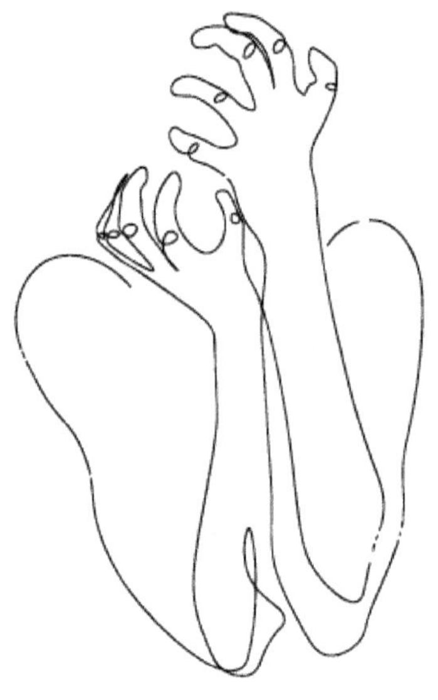

Yin-Yang

I can run as hot as lava
Or as cool as the tundra.

I can be as solid as stone
Or formless as water.

I can be as immovable as a fortress
Or as springy as a gel.

The desert heat beating on your head or the
spring breeze caressing your face.

The wild storm or the relaxed sky.

The knife in the heart or the shield on the back.

The creator of chaos or the preserver of peace.

The either and the other.

The neither and the all.

I am discord; I am balance.

I am light; I am dark.

I am human life.

I am a Yin-Yang

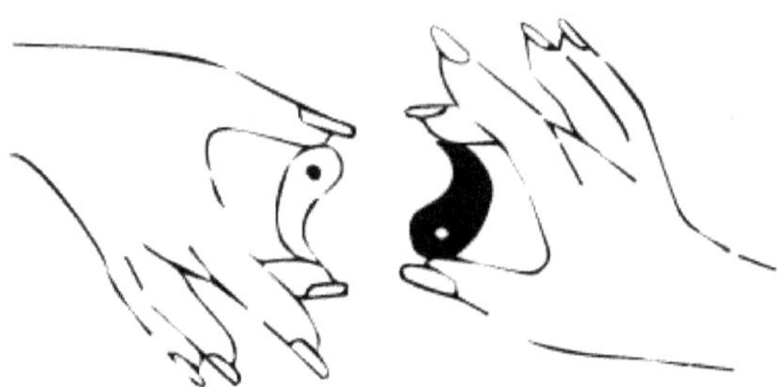

Get up

Breathing heavy...
Body aching...
Sweat pouring...

Gotta get up.

Weapon beside me...
Little out of reach...
The sky Is burning...

Gotta get up.

Battle all around me...
Weapons clashing...
Sounds of people dying...

Gotta get up.

The air's hot...
Hard to breathe...
Eyes getting heavy...Darkness

Gotta get up.

Someone is calling me...

Who's calling me?.
They're calling me...

Gotta get up...

They are calling me to rise...

Gotta get up.

To stand...

Gotta get up.

To fight!

Gotta get up.
Gotta get up!

"Hey, sleepyhead...you got to get up!"

Hero and villian

No one wakes up wanting to be a hero or a villain.

No, both of these people just wanted change.

They wanted to change their station.

Change their life.

Change their world.

So it must be the tactics, right?

Villains use force; heroes use words.

Think about how much media, stories, legends.

Have the hero use the same tactics as the villain.

Even the more violent tactics at times.

The villain is oppressive and doesn't care about who they hurt.

The hero has slain many henchmen, bosses, and
minions. Most probably trying to follow the
status quo.

Maybe it's in their origin.

They had their home burned down.

The world beat them down.

They lost family.

They were slaves.

They were abused.

They didn't hurt anymore.

They wanted to change their life.

They turned their agony to power.

They broke through and made their oath.

Who?

Who am I talking about?

The hero who's praised?

Th villain who's feared?

What action inflicted them with either title?

And when you go out to change the world?

What title will you be branded with?

Cause no one genuinely wants to be a hero or villain.

They just want a change.

All has been said

Tut-tut
All has been said
The day is done
Make sure you're fed.

Tut-tut
All has been said
You did well today
Relax your head.

Tut-tut
All has been said
With the raised moon
You need to stop soon.

Tut-tut
All has been said
Stop reading these lines
And close your eyes.

Tut-tut
All has been said
Try to ignore
This poem words

Tut-tut
All have been told
Your need to read
Won't end pleasantly

Tut-tut
All has been said
I don't want the end
Stop this, my friend

Tut-tut
All has been said
You have been warned
Do not read on.

Tut-tut
All has been said...

Tut-tut
All has been said.....

Tut-tut
Tut-tut
Tut-tut
All has been said...

YOU IGNORED MY WORDS!
GIVE ME YOUR HEA-!

Courage

What is courage?

Some would say it's not being scared.

It is being fearless in the face of anything.

Sure, that what it looks like... But that's wrong.

Fear can give way to caution, and it's good to be a little cautious.

Ok, it's overcoming your fear, being bigger than you fear.

That's wrong cause it takes courage to do that.

So what is courage?

Waking up every morning without motivation.

Smiling knowing that some wish harm on you.

Enjoying and living your truth despite what the world says.

Accepting defeats and victories in the capacity.

Knowing what you can and can't change.

Making the changes for your betterment.

Allowing yourself to tear up...

Curl up...

Break down and release all you held back.

So you can stand ready for the next wave of life.

This is courage.

Living this human experience is courage.

Your human experience is a testament to courage.

Don't ever think less of it.

Ifirt and Icy

He runs as hot as the August heat.
Excitable, energetic, impulsive.
He was a star, a supernova, an undying sun of
honest emotion that he wished to share with the
world.

She runs cold as the November winds.
Calm, cunning, calculated.
She was a glacier, an arctic plain, unshakable,
steady ice of love, and undeniable valor, which
only the luckiest get to experience.

 Their opposing features were always on display

Their conflicting attributes showed in their
actions, their speech... Their body temperatures.

And they adored each other for it.

The Ifrit of heat loved her steely precision and
controlled poise, even when she's ranting.

How centered she is even during the most
daunting of moments.

How her sly smile, as small as it was, held that unbreakable love only she possessed and was able to give.

The spirit of ice was enamored by Ifrits' unrelenting passion for life.

How even in the darkest of times, he remained a burning flame of power and motivation.

How his eyes always held a heated flicker of excitement, even in his most serene moments.

Ifrit loves her blue touch on his red skin.

How it felt like a lovely cool spring running along him.

 Her hugs were a pleasant calming shade against the heat.

Her gentle whispers were the best winter wind.

Her kisses, a refreshing drink from the most beautiful oasis ever created.

Icy, she was never too physical with her care, going for more verbal cues...Except for ifrit.

He ran hotter than anyone else, and she found herself addicted.

His hugs were a warm blanket. His cuddling nuzzles a summer day.

His chuckles were the spring breeze, and his lips were the most gentle, body-warming tea alive.

She was the cool that kept him from burning himself out.

He was the heat that kept her from freezing up.

Together, they were an everlasting and complimentary warmth, known as love.

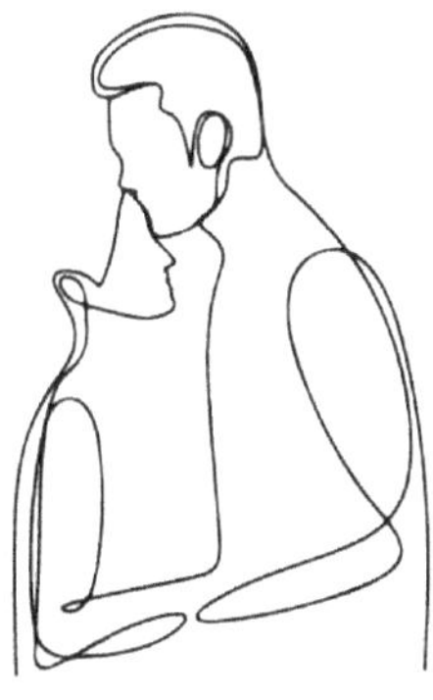

A moment

A moment is all it takes.

All it takes to.

Breath in.

Compose yourself.

De-stress.

Exhale.

Formulate.

Gather your strength.

Hold on to it tight.

Ignite it.

Jump into it.

Knead into it

Let it

Mold you.

Nudge you.

Open you.

Push you.

Quake your soul.

Shake it.

Tremble it.

Unlock it.

Vigorously,

With newfound power

'Xuding.

Your eyes open and feet planted.

Zoom toward your challenge and victory

Where she wants to be

The television blared as it played an episode of Buccano, the jazzy theme opening making hum in tune.

She's where she wants to be.

Her smile was relaxed as she lay down. The warmth under her head was greatly welcomed. It was far too long since she felt it.

She's where she wants to be.

She sighed in pleasure. She could finally unwind. No work needed to be done. Summer was here, so school was closed, and her work-study at the labs was going smoothly, and so was his, which made her smile.

She didn't have to worry about him or worry him.

She's where she wants to be.

She heard him chuckle and hummed quizzically
from above but didn't respond to happy having
him as a lap pillow, watching an exciting anime
about immortal mafioso.

"Hey"

His gentle voice warmed her heart as his
calloused fingers brushed her hair delicately.

"Hmm?" She turned to face him with a gentle
smile. She was playfully nuzzling into his hand
once it caressed her cheek.

"The others are meeting at Karaoke. Wanted to
know if we're going to join?"

She looked at him and shook his head before
kissing his palm.

"I'm right where I want to be."

Worth it

She giggled as I sat her on the table, which was
soon interrupted by a pair of lips.
Chap and plump compared to her own.
Her sighs became hums as the kiss deepened.

His tongue teasingly brushes against my teeth
and gums in a slow sensual massage.
My nerves flared in response.
My heart drummed as sparks ran through her.
My legs locked him in place and pressed his
belly to my pelvis.

I feel his right hand on my shoulder in a secure
grip.
His left slipped and squeezed the seat of my
shorts.

"Ye~MMMM~MM!"

She was interrupted as my tongue made it pass
her moan
caressing her own.

The feel of our breaths becoming one.
Our tongues, twisting in an exploratory dance.

Our moans in a delicious duet.

It made me crave him.
It made me yearn for her.

Her right hand found my scalp, pulling me close.
Her left steadied herself as she went on the
offensive.

Hearing him moan and feeling his right hand
join his left on my ass evoked and turned my
inner sparks into embers.

I break the kiss to return to the minors, teasing
nips.

Once...Twice...Thrice...

The slightly surprised yet hungrily lovestruck
look they gave me said it all.

With a nod, I am lifted by him, hands kneading
my seat as he carries me to the stairs.

She looked down at me before giving me a kiss,
tender and loving.

"I love you."

He smiled tearfully before kissing me back.

Moments like this made everything else worth it.

The only one

She wanted to rage,
to scream,
to burn it all down and start back to one,
but she couldn't.

It wouldn't be right for her or fair to him.

She didn't have the luxury of swearing never to
love the child or man who took
Rita away.

The will to be done with it all and leave it, leave
them all like Amy.

The audacity to claim everything was a lie and
rejected everything and everyone away like
Saph.

OR The 'luck' to be killed like George.

No, someone had to be here, to be the caretaker
for the little boy who had crime was birth

Fate chose her.

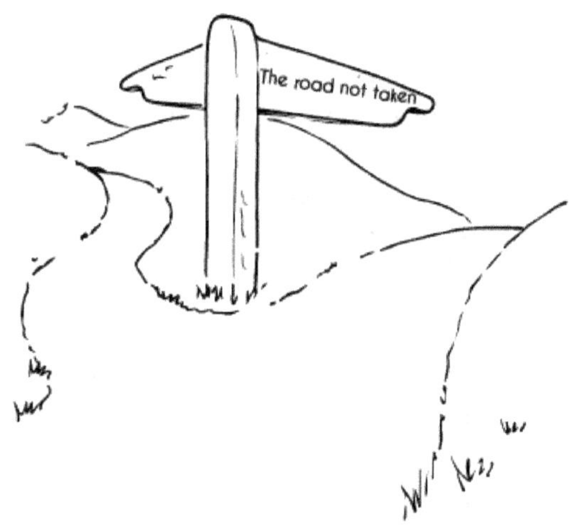

The road not taken

Freedom

She didn't care at all.

She didn't care about the looks of her classmates.

Didn't care about the crumbled and bloody body
of her bully.

Not about the screaming, commanding boom of
the principal voice.

Not about talk of legal action.

Of the blood splattered on the left of her face,
the split on her lip,
  scratch above her eye.

As she sat with an arched brow and the smallest
of smirks, she realized.

She didn't care a bit about the consequences.

She was finally free.

The end

It comes to this...
We all knew it was coming...
We were warned of it two months prior.

Our final days.
Our exodus.
Our Apocalypse.
The end of everything.

Some are running for their lives, meaningless.
Some are looking for their family, precious.
Some are engaged in last-minute debauchery,
understandable.
Some found god and are trying to secure
salvation, also understandable.

Some are trying to live today like any other.
And then you got me.

Whose walking the last cobbled road, he will
walk.
Reminiscing on the life he had..and what a life it
was.

How were we even warned about the end?
It was...Television?
What is television?
My head began to ache again...

Doesn't matter.
Wat does matter is who I am.

An innkeeper that is what I am.
A damn good one.
Met many travelers during my time.

Most prominent in my mind was this party of
four.
Said they were gonna change the world. Don't
really remember much about what we talked
about or ate.
Though, I do remember their stay.

For some reason, I can not think of other guests.
I had the place for years; many stopped and rest.

But all I remember is my inn and those four.
As if they were my whole world.

I have an entire life.
A child...a Wife.

Their names are...

Their names are...
Their names are... Zamasu, Izkiel, Kelly, Brice.

No...No that the names of the four.

What is the name of my wife and child?
Innkeeper wife.
Innkeeper child.

And my name..
Oh.. My name...
is innkeeper.

I keep an inn.
A character with no story
Only an end.

Meaning

"What is the meaning of life?"

A grandparent was asked of their grandchild.

They smile as they think back to their own life.

The friendships they forged, The food they ate.

The time they stole from the store to pay for a date.

The smiles of their parents and peers, the times they witnessed genuine fears.

The heartbreaks they caused, the heartbreaks they felt.

The bed partners they made fall and melt.

Those who doubted their success and those who shouted for their success.

The wars, the struggles, the battles.

Both inner and outer,

physical, mental, and emotional.

The failures, the defeats, the setbacks.

The wins, the victories, the triumphs.

Both their own and those they witnessed.

The lessons from both.

The change from both.

The ever continuous change.

In people, in culture, in society, in themselves.

In observing birth, in living life, in witnessing death, and accepting that it's all connected and continuous.

How all of it... Every...Second of it.

Every decision. Every result. Every fault. Every feat.

Everything led up to this question from the child in front of them.

A whole world of endless possibilities, yet
learned lessons, missteps, and accomplishments
in their eyes.

With a wise and excited grin, they answer.

"Experience."